4208

FIELD ATHLETICS

Adrianne Blue

WORLD OF SPORT

American Football	**Judo**
Basketball	**Rugby**
Cricket	**Soccer**
Field athletics	**Swimming and Diving**
Fishing	**Tennis**
Gymnastics	**Track athletics**

Editor: Tim Byrne

Cover: Fatima Whitbread (GB) winning the Javelin World Championships in 1987.

First published in 1988 by
Wayland (Publishers) Ltd
61 Western Road, Hove
East Sussex BN3 1JD, England

British Library Cataloguing
in Publication Data
Blue, Adrianne   Field
athletics. – (World of sport).
  1. Athletics – Juvenile
literature
  I. Title   II. Series
  796.4′2   GV1060.5

ISBN 1–85210–316–7

Printed and bound in Italy
by Sagdos

Phototypeset and designed by
DP Press Ltd, Sevenoaks, Kent

Picture acknowledgements:
All pictures supplied by
ALL SPORT(UK) LTD
(except 5, Ronald Sheridan)
All artwork by Peter Parr

Author's dedication: Lyn
Allison, my friend and first
coach

Contents

This book can be used with WORLD OF SPORT: Track athletics

History of field athletics

Field athletics are all the jumping and throwing events that take place on the field in the centre of an athletics track. There are eight field events and these can be divided into two categories:

1 **Jumping**
- High jump
- Long jump
- Triple jump
- Pole vault

2 **Throwing**
- Javelin
- Shot Put
- Discus
- Hammer

Each field athletic event has developed differently throughout history, and it is only in recent times that they have all been brought together in championships and in the Olympics.

In 1896 the Olympic Games were started up again at Athens, Greece in this stadium. The last time the ancient Olympics were held was in AD 394.

Stone-casting, as the shot put was called in its early days, had become very popular during the reign of Edward III. Instead of concentrating on archery practice, the army wasted hours stone casting. The king banned the sport in 1365. The shot put actually started in Ireland, at the thirty-day Talietean Games, held every year in County Meath, from 1829 BC until the Norman invasion in AD 1168.

Other field events are even older. Pole vaulting was devised by a distant ancestor. When there was no bridge, he or she used a long pole to vault across a stream. It could also be used to jump over chasms or across burning fires. In Africa, long before the ancient Olympics of Greece, they uscd to have high jumping competitions.

In ancient Greek mythology there are many stories about great athletes. One story tells of Atalanta, a young woman, who grew up in the wilderness where she learned to run and hunt using a javelin. She went out with a number of hunters to track down a dangerous wild boar. The competition to kill the boar was fierce, but hers was the first javelin that struck.

Throwing the discus was one of the main events at the ancient Olympic Games. When the Olympics were revived in 1896, the discus was an event the modern Greeks were determined to win. They studied the famous classical statue called *Discobolus* for technique. A Greek did win the marathon race, but an American university student won the discus.

The ruins of the stadium at Delphi, Greece, one of the sites of the Ancient Olympic Games.

In 1928, at the Olympic Games field event debut, women competed in the discus and high jump. At the next Olympics, in Los Angeles in 1932, Mildred 'Babe' Didrikson became the most talked about athlete at the Games. She was a great all-rounder and won gold medals in the javelin and hurdles race, setting a new hurdles world record in the process. In the high jump, she was awarded a silver medal but shared in the world record with the gold medallist. Both jumped exactly the same height but Didrikson had had more failures at the earlier heights.

The 1932 Los Angeles Olympics were the first to have an Olympic village for athletes. They were also the first Olympics to make a big profit for the organizers. At the 1936 Berlin Olympics, which became known as the Nazi Olympics, Adolf Hitler tried to promote his racist ideas through the success of the German athletes. They were very good, but the black American Jesse Owens won four gold medals and set an 8.13 m world long jump record. He was the star of the Games.

At the 1968 Olympics in Mexico City, which is high above sea level, came one of the most amazing moments of athletics history. A tall New Yorker named Bob Beamon long jumped 8.9 m, this was over 60 cm longer than the previous record. He was competing under perfect conditions for the event – with the aid of the maximum allowable wind and at a high altitude, which is also a help.

Mildred 'Babe' Didrikson (USA) won the javelin and 80m hurdles at the 1932 Los Angeles Olympics.

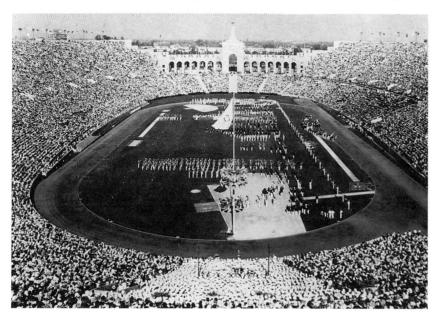

The Coliseum at Los Angeles (USA) where the 1932 and 1984 Olympic Games were held.

Bob Beamon (USA) breaking the world long jump record at the 1968 Mexico Olympics with a leap of 8.90m (29'2½").

Jumpers have been trying to beat his remarkable record ever since.

The East Germans now arrived at the centre stage of world athletics and produced a number of star performers. The women, especially, did well. One reason these *wunderfrauen* (wonderwomen) were so successful was that the Germans did not think hard training was unfeminine. Neither did other countries in the Eastern bloc. Soon the West realized the East was right about this, and girls and women in the USA and Western Europe began to train more seriously for their events. When the East German Ruth Fuchs won the gold medal in the javelin at the 1976 Olympics, few could foresee that it would be two British women who would succeed her as the world stars. Tessa Sanderson and Fatima Whitbread have dominated the event in the 1980s.

Sergey Bubka (USSR) has used new training methods to break records in the pole vault event.

Large male athletes from the Eastern bloc countries were the first to use new methods of training and they have made important contributions to field athletics. The Russian athlete, Sergey Bubka, revolutionized the pole vault.

Unfortunately, politics has always intruded on sport. The Olympic Games were cancelled for the duration of the Second World War. At the 1972 Games, Israeli athletes were murdered by terrorists.

In 1980, the United States and many other Western nations boycotted the Moscow Olympics. In 1984 some Eastern bloc countries boycotted the Los Angeles Olympics. Even so, athletes of all nations continue to enjoy competing together. They enjoy learning better techniques from other athletes and they play by the same rules wherever they come from.

Recent developments

Television

Two-and-a-half billion people had their eyes focused on the long jump pit when Carl Lewis went for gold at the 1984 Los Angeles Olympics. Nowhere near that many would fit into the Coliseum. Fortunately, they were able to watch his victory via satellite television. Millions of people who have

Carl Lewis (USA) won four gold medals at the 1984 Los Angeles Olympics. He also became a well-known personality internationally due to the worldwide coverage of the Olympics on television.

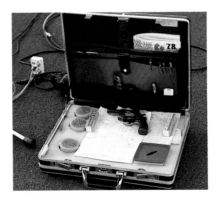

Starting equipment. The starting pistol is linked electronically to the automatic timing equipment to gain an accurate timing.

This equipment measures the wind speed in the athletics stadium. Wind speed can affect an athletes performance.

never been to a stadium now watch athletics on television. It has brought athletics to a much bigger audience.

Television has also taught us to rely on the clever invention of the action replay. If you miss something important during the competition, you can see it again. This was not possible before the camera arrived at the stadium. Television is a surprisingly recent development. The 1960 Olympic Games in Rome were the first to be televised worldwide. Television has brought its own and the sponsors' money into athletics. As a result many world-ranked athletes have become famous and rich.

Timing and Measurement

Timing is much more accurate now than it used to be. Automatic timing devices linked electronically to the starting pistol start the clock at the instant the trigger is pressed. Until the 1950s, there was always a brief delay before the timing was started, because it was done by hand. This was called manual timekeeping. The timekeeper would start his watch as soon as he saw the smoke from the starting pistol. Some timekeepers were faster at this than others so the times were often inaccurate. Automatic timekeeping was then introduced as a backup. Now manual timing is used as backup.

The wind speed is another factor. There is equipment placed around the stadium to record the wind speed during each event. If the wind is more than 2m/sec any record that is set during the event will not be official.

Drug Abuse

Athletes are always training to be bigger and stronger. To achieve this more quickly, some have taken drugs to build up their muscles. This is not only cheating, but also dangerous to the athletes' health. Anabolic steroids are the drugs which have been used most. They are illegal in sport. They are synthetic male hormones which can increase weight. They can also enable athletes to train longer hours so that they can get stronger more quickly. But they can have dangerous side-effects such as acne and cancer. If athletes are caught taking them they are supposed to be banned from their event. Growth hormone is another illegal drug which may have short-term benefits but which is also very dangerous.

There is random drug-testing at all major competitions and at many small ones. These tests are having some effect on drug-taking at international level, but drug-taking is still a major problem. Now that the tests for drugs are very thorough, it is likely that those cheating will have to give up the drugs or else give up their sport – unless they are caught first and thrown out.

Electronic timing equipment gives an accurate and immediate result of a race.

Open Athletics

At one time only amateurs were allowed to compete in athletics. Amateurs were athletes who did not accept any money for competing. As the world standard went up, top competitors found they had to train full-time to stay competitive. Many also had to earn a living, but all they had time for, and all they had trained for, was athletics. Yet getting paid for sport was against the rules of amateurism. Many athletes accepted payments secretly. They didn't know what else they could do. Amateurism began to be a sham. The first sign of 'shamateurism' came when the great

US decathlete, Jim Thorpe, was stripped of his two 1912 gold medals because he had played professional baseball. Forty-

This vest worn by triple jumper Willie Banks (USA) shows the name of three sponsors. Sponsors give money to athletes to help with their training. In return the athletes display the sponsors' name on their clothes during competition.

one years later, when the attitudes toward amateur sport had changed, his amateur status was restored.

The first female shamateur we know of was the great Babe Didrikson. She was employed by an insurance company, supposedly as a typist, but her salary was really for playing basketball for the winning company team and for training for the 1932 Olympics where the insurance company paid her way.

In 1982, the IAAF (International Amateur Athletics Federation) ended this problem by agreeing that athletes could be paid openly for sponsorship and advertising deals. The following year, the IAAF also agreed that they could receive appearance money. Usually, the money goes into trust funds from which only expenses are drawn until the athlete ends his or her career. This new state of affairs in which athletes can earn money is called open athletics. It has put an end to the hypocrisy of 'shamateurism'.

The life of a professional athlete

Daley Thompson

Daley Thompson has been one of the most consistent athletes in the world in the hardest event of all – the decathlon. He has been the Olympic, World and European champion. He was born in July 1958, and between 1978 and 1986 did not lose a single competition. The decathlon is an event that lasts for two days and combines both field and track events. It consists of the long jump, high jump, pole vault, 100 m, 400 m, 1,500 m, 110 m hurdles, shot put, discus and javelin.

Every time Daley Thompson enters a decathlon he has to produce a peak performance not just once, but ten times. He also has to train for all those events. No athlete has more to do than a decathlete.

Daley Thompson (GB) needs to be good at ten events to win the decathlon. The high jump is one of the decathlon events.

The decathlon involves four track events. Daley Thompson (GB) trained hard at 100m, 400m and 1,500m and 110m hurdles to win decathlon championships.

Daley Thompson (GB) needs strength in both his arms and legs to win decathlon events. You can see the power of his arms as he throws the javelin.

Thompson's physique is powerful. The strength, agility and endurance of his 1.86 m, broad-shouldered body are phenomenal. The little boy who gave into every impulse, who played aimlessly in the streets of London, disciplined himself into becoming a walking, talking decathlon machine. Whether he is training in California where he is based, or at his home in England, his routine continues.

'My life consists of going from the track to my bed,' he says. 'But I'm lucky. With all these sports, I spend most of my life enjoying something that most people only manage in their spare time.'

Daley is lucky too that when he was only seven, his energetic attention-seeking was channelled into sport. He was sent to a school for difficult boys which was very sports orientated. Daley's mother was white, and his father was black. When he won at sports – which was most of the time – he was no longer sneered at by bullies because he was the only black pupil in the school. Instead he was applauded.

His father died when Daley was thirteen. Concentrating on sport helped him bear the grief. He started training to become England's fastest sprinter but a coach directed him to the decathlon. At nineteen, Daley was an Olympic athlete. He was already very self-disciplined, willing to attend carefully to every detail of his training and to sacrifice a great deal to it. He once lunched with the Queen, but he refused another royal invitation, saying he would be out of town. He was at home relaxing between training sessions.

Undeterred by the weather, dedicated athletes like Daley Thompson (GB) try their very hardest to win every time they compete.

Athletes encounter defeat at some point in their careers. Daley Thompson (GB) went for over eight years before being beaten.

Seven hours of training, seven days a week are necessary to keep athletes like Daley at the top. He spends a lot of that time on the track. He builds up his leg muscles with bounding exercises while wearing a weighted jacket. These are *callisthenics* for suppleness. Weight training develops his upper body. There has to be a balance between strength and building up too much muscle bulk which might reduce his speed. Extra weight may help him in the throwing events but won't help in events such as the 1500 m.

In the discus, the trick, he says, is to rotate your body like a screw. He throws well for a decathlete, but his best is about 6 m shorter than a champion who specialized in the discus would do. A decathlete is a superb all-rounder, but he can rarely become as good in individual events as the athletes who specialize in them.

The emphasis of his training changes, as does every top athlete's, with the season. Your athletics coach will know about this. He or she will also know of many of the drills Daley uses to improve in each of his events.

A good decathlete has to have height for jumping, weight and strength for throwing, speed for track events, and endurance to get through all of it. Daley has them all.

The stars

Bob Beamon

The New Yorker who set an 'unbeatable' long jump record. See the entry below about Carl Lewis. (See p.7 for picture)

Sergey Bubka

Soviet athletes head the world-best lists in the pole vault, high jump, and long jump, and in each case an American is ranked second. The Russian Sergey Bubka transformed the pole vault event. In Paris, in July 1985, when he was only 21, Bubka broke the psychological barrier for pole vaulters of 6 m (19ft 8¼ in), setting a new world record.

Heike Dreschler (GDR) broke the world long jump record in 1985.

Heike Dreschler

She is the current East German *wunderfrau*, an accomplished long jumper, and more. She has been world champion and, in Berlin in 1985, she set a new world long jump record of 7.44 m. The previous record had belonged to Anisoara Cusmir Stanciu of Romania.

Mildred 'Babe' Didrikson

At the Los Angeles Olympics in 1932, Mildred Didrikson, who liked to be called 'Babe' after a famous baseball player (Babe Ruth), was the star of the Games. This tough Texan, who was only 19, won Olympic medals in throwing, running and jumping events – gold in the javelin and hurdles, but only silver in the high jump after a controversial decision to declare her 'Western' roll style of jumping illegal at the end of the competition. Although Babe was awarded only a silver medal but shared in the world record with the gold medallist, even though both had jumped exactly the same height. Babe was a gifted all-rounder, good at basketball, swimming, tennis and baseball. She was probably the first female 'shamateur'. After she married, she was called Babe Didrikson Zaharias. She became a champion pro-golf player, and is considered the finest female athlete of the first half of this century. (See p.6 for picture)

Jurgen Hingsen

This West German decathlete was born in 1958; he is 1.98m
and weighs 97 kg. Hingsen's best events are the shot and
discus, the high jump, where his height helps, and the
1,500 m.

Jurgen Hingsen (FDR), a decathlete,
clears the high-jump.

Uwe Hohn

The East German whose gigantic javelin throw of 104.8 m
(343 feet, ten inches) may stand forever as a world record.
After he set it, in Berlin in 1984, the design of javelins was
changed so they do not now go as far.

Carl Lewis (USA) came near to the world record for the long jump in 1981. As he landed here, he was 27cm short of breaking Bob Beamon's 1968 record.

Carl Lewis

When he was just 19, in the summer of 1981, Carl Lewis came to the world's notice. He came within 27 cm of Bob Beamon's 'untouchable' 1968 world long jump record. Bob Beamon, a gangling New Yorker, had set that mark assisted by the maximum allowable wind and by the thin air of Mexico City. Lewis also ran the 100 m faster than anyone ever had at sea level.

Two years later he leaped even further, with a long jump of 8.79 m, the best ever at sea level. At that time it was second only to Beamon's jump at altitude. He also ran the 200 m faster than anyone ever had at sea level. He won three gold medals at the first world athletics championships, including one in the long jump, and at the 1984 Olympics he won the long jump gold medal.

Sport runs in his family. Carl Lewis's mother and sister have competed internationally – his mother Evelyn as a sprint hurdler, his sister Carol as a long jumper. Lewis's brother Cleve has played pro-soccer, and their father Bill has been a sports teacher.

Jesse Owens

Jesse Owens was the tenth child of a poor, black Southern sharecropper, but at 22, he became the idol of millions. At the 1936 Berlin Olympics, which Hitler's Third Reich had wanted to turn into a racist propaganda event, Jesse Owens won four Olympic gold medals including the long jump. He was the star of the Games. The year before, in Michigan, Owens had raised the world long jump record by six inches to 26ft 8¼in (8.13 m). This record remained unbeaten for a quarter of a century – 25 years and 79 days to be exact – when Ralph Boston set the new world record in 1960.

Heidi Rosendahl (FDR) winning the gold medal in the long jump at the 1972 Olympics at Munich, Germany.

Heidi Rosendahl

Heidi Rosendahl's father was a world-ranked discus thrower, but this German girl took to the long jump and the track. She broke the world long jump record in 1970 and two years later, at the 1972 Olympics, won gold. Her other Olympic medals were in the pentathlon and the relay. She was a great all-rounder.

Tessa Sanderson (GB) about to win the javelin gold medal at the 1984 Los Angeles Olympics, USA.

Tessa Sanderson

One of the two great female javelin throwers in Britain, Tessa Sanderson became the Olympic champion at Los Angeles in 1984. She had been the British champion for years, but had never done as well in international competition. She grew up in Birmingham, in England, although she was born in Jamaica.

Anisoara Cusmir Stanciu

The long jump world record holder for many years, but would this Romanian athlete have become the 1984 Olympic champion if Heike Dreschler had been at the Games, which were boycotted by the East Germans?

Anisora Cusmir Stanciu (Romania) won the long jump gold medal at the 1984 Los Angeles Olympics, USA.

Fatima Whitbread

In an empty stadium in Stuttgart, during the qualifying round of the 1986 European Championship, this British woman set a new javelin world record. She was 25, the first Briton of either sex ever to set a world record in a field event, and the first woman in the world to throw more than 250 ft (76.64 m). She went on to win the European Championships and in 1987 she won the gold medal at the World Championships in Rome.

Throwing events

You can usually tell who the throwers are in any group of athletes. They are normally the heaviest ones, with hefty shoulders and biceps and big, muscular thighs. Strength is just as important in throwing as technique. Good technique is crucial and learning it can be tricky. Some people think it is harder to pick up the skills of the four throwing events – javelin, shot put, discus, and hammer – than it is to learn the simpler ones of running.

Javelin

Javelin competitions usually take place at the same time as track events. The standard of javelin throwing improved so much in the 1980s that officials worried that a runner might be speared. When East Germany's Uwe Hohn set a new

Fatima Whitbread (GB) was the first Briton to set a world record in a field event in 1986 when she set a new javelin world record.

Jackie Joyner-Kersee (USA) displays a good technique in throwing the javelin. You can see how her arms are parallel ready to throw the javelin over her right shoulder.

world record with a gigantic throw of 104.80 m, officials decided to change the specifications of the javelin. Now javelins are designed so they will not go as far. That world record Uwe Hohn set in Berlin, in the summer of 1984, may stand forever. Unlike the other throwing events, javelin throwing is a straight-line event, and is a lot like throwing a tennis ball. You need a strong shoulder and arm to throw the ball, but the javelin requires a more exact technique.

The event itself dates back to ancient Greece when the army would spend hours practising their spear throwing. Today's javelin is really a very modern kind of spear. Throwing it requires the most all-round fitness of any throwing event. This is because you need speed and mobility, as well as strength and technique. In competition, a javelin thrower runs fast up to a chalked line, and hurls the javelin as far as possible.

The run-up is absolutely essential to the throw. Top class throwers usually take between eight to twelve strides. Most of them pull back their throwing arm four strides before the

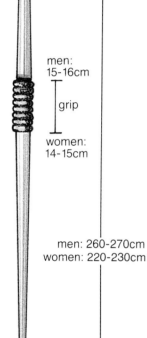

men:
15-16cm

grip

women:
14-15cm

men: 260-270cm
women: 220-230cm

25-33cm

Javelins are precisely engineered
pieces of equipment and therefore have
to be stored carefully.

final moment of delivery, and on the last stride bring their arm through fast for the throw. You throw the javelin over your shoulder. Your final stride should put plenty of power into the throw, using your torso and legs for leverage. You usually end up hopping on one foot.

The instant when you actually let go of the javelin is called the moment of release. This moment has to be explosive because once the javelin has been released there is nothing more you can do to help it take flight.

The javelin has to land point first, and make a mark in the turf, but it doesn't have to actually stick in the ground. A judge measures the throw to the nearest centimetre. If the javelin has landed flat and made no mark, it is not considered a valid throw nor is the throw counted if the thrower has stepped over the scratch line at the end of the run-up.

At the Olympics, or any other major competition, athletes take turns throwing. Every athlete takes one throw, then in the second round every athlete takes another, and so on. Each athlete gets six throws, unless there are more than eight competitors in an event. Then, everybody takes three throws, and the best eight competitors get three more. At big events you have to qualify in a separate round for the final.

Shot Put

The shot is shaped like a cannonball. It has a smooth surface, and its weight depends on your age. The minimum weight is 3.2 kg while the senior men's shot weighs 7.2 kg.

The most efficient way to throw such a heavy an object is to *put* it. What this amounts to is pushing it from above your shoulder. You hold the shot with one hand, close to your

Connie Polman-Tuin (Canada) twists her body around in order to push the shot away from herself.

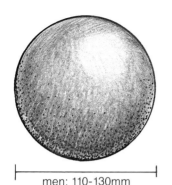

men: 110-130mm

minimum weight: 7.26kg (16lb)

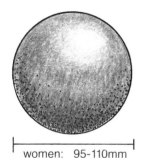

women: 95-110mm

minimum weight: 4kg (8lb 13oz)

Men's and women's shot puts with dimensions.

The shot puts are stored in racks between throws.

chin. You must throw from the shoulder, and never let your hand get any lower than chin level. Many shot putters say they can feel when they have thrown well.

The shot is put from a concrete circle. A wooden stopboard in front of the circle helps the athlete from falling forwards out of the circle, but they must not step over it once they have thrown or their throw will not be measured.

The back-facing O'Brien technique is the most widely used method of putting the shot. The thrower stands at the rear of the circle with his or her back to the direction of the throw, whirls around, and pushes the shot off. This technique is named after Parry O'Brien, the American shot putter who first used it. O'Brien was unbeaten for an unprecedented 116 contests between 1952 and 1956, and was the 1952 Olympic champion.

Like the newer Baryshnikov technique, the O'Brien uses the strongest muscles of the body first, those in the legs, and then it goes on to use the faster arm movements.

All throwers need to train for technique, speed, mobility and strength. A good way to build strength is to train with weights. Serious adult athletes put in three sessions of weight training a week during the winter and spring.

The Baryshnikov put is named after the Russian shot putter Aleksandr Baryshnikov who was the first to use it. Baryshnikov was good enough to represent his country at the 1972 Olympics, and two years later, he set a European record of 21.7 m. His method, which requires more rotation of the body than the O'Brien, is a lot like discus throwing.

In competition, putters have three rounds of throws. Then the best eight putters get three more.

You need weight training to build up strength for this event, and to practice the basic puts. You can practice the full put without the shot until you are happy with the movement. Skip jumping on the spot with your arms extended in front of you is another exercise you can do.

A count taken after the 1984 Los Angeles Olympics showed that American shot putters had won 15 Olympic gold medals since the Games began. At seven of the Games, they had won every medal going. But the East German Udo Beyer has been setting world records since 1978.

(Above) Jackie Joyner-Kersee (USA) shows the concentration needed to achieve a best performance.

(Left) You can see Jackie's body lift from the ground as she whirls around pushing the shot with her whole body.

Discus

The discus looks like a flying saucer. It is a round disc which is fatter in the middle than at the edges. It is heavy too, yet despite its space age look, the discus has a very long history. It was one of the main events at the Olympic Games in ancient Greece. To throw the discus you grip it with the spread-eagled fingers of one hand, and you spin around the stone circle with it in your hand. The discus is released when the body is spinning at its fastest, with the arm held straight. This is all done in one continuous movement. Ideally, the discus will spin away from your first finger on a steady and balanced trajectory.

Imrich Buga (Czechoslovakia) twists forward with his left arm and follows through the action with his right arm held straight.

Between throws the discuses are stored on a special table and are carefully cleaned and polished ready for the next athlete.

(Below and right) Al Oerter (USA) is one of the greatest discus throwers ever. He won four consecutive Olympic gold medals between 1956–68. Each time he was either ranked as an outsider or came from a long way behind to win.

The further the discus is from your body during the turn, the faster it is travelling, and the further it is likely to go when you release it. A long, loose throwing arm helps. For safety's sake, the concrete throwing circle is surrounded by a wire cage shaped like the letter 'C'. As in other throwing events, you get three rounds of throws, and the best eight competitors then get three throws more.

Many discus throwers train with weights to build up their strength. They also need plenty of practice in all phases of the throw, with and without the discus in their hand. The most famous discus thrower ever was Al Oerter, an American who not only held world records but won the Olympic title four times between 1956 and 1968. The most renowned woman discus thrower was Liesel Westerman of West Germany. She opened the way for fast and strong female throwers like the great Faina Melnik of the USSR, who set eleven world records and became the first thrower, male or female, to throw a discus more than 70 m.

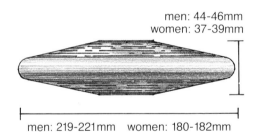

men: 44-46mm
women: 37-39mm

men: 219-221mm   women: 180-182mm

Men's and women's discuses with dimensions.

Hammer

A hammer thrower has to be careful because the hammer can be a lethal weapon. As the thrower you are responsible for making sure no one is in danger when you throw. Like the discus, the hammer is thrown from within a concrete circle surrounded by a wire cage, and the best eight competitors get an extra three throws. Unlike the discus, it has a short history, dating from 1887 – before then, long-handled mallets were used. The head of the hammer used in the sport today is really a round metal ball. This is attached

From within a wire cage the hammer thrower spins and turns to build up speed before letting the hammer fly.

to a length of flexible wire, which has a hand grip attached at the end.

You use both hands to hold onto the hammer, and if you want to, you may wear a glove. This is not allowed in the other throwing events. It is best to give the hammer a few preliminary swings and then pivot in a full circle about three times on one foot, with a push-off from the other leg at each turn. In the first section of the turn, you are pivoting on your heel, and in the second part on the ball of your foot. The hammer moves faster as you turn. It has to be going fast before you let go, or it will not fly very far. The object is to get

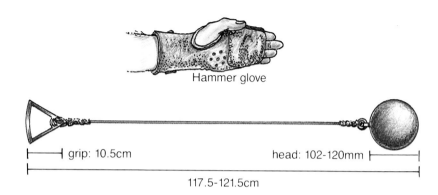

Hammer glove

grip: 10.5cm   head: 102-120mm

117.5-121.5cm

A hammer and glove with dimensions.

an explosive release so that the long wire and hammer go up and away with a whiplash effect. It helps to swing the hammer in the biggest possible arc. A good way of achieving this big arc, or sweep, is to hold your arms quite straight at the elbow when you are swinging the hammer. This also keeps it well away from your body. You try to get your hips ahead of your shoulders, and your shoulders ahead of the hammer, until the moment you let go. Unless you learn to do this, even if you can turn quickly, you will not be able to throw very far.

When practising the heel-toe turns without a hammer you should concentrate on balance. You will need to practise the swing too. Then combine the turn and the swing in drills to learn to have balance and rhythm at the same time. Training with weights will increase your strength. Most of the world's best hammer throwers come from the Soviet Union, where it is taken very seriously as a sport. The hammer event is not yet open to women.

Jumping events

There are four jumping events in field athletics: the high jump, the triple jump, the long jump and the pole vault.

You need plenty of athletic ability for these four events. You need patience too because in competition you have to wait for your turn to come round, no matter how eager you are to go for a better jump. This has advantages too. You rest between jumps and may find yourself getting better and better as you warm up during the competition.

High Jump

In a sense, the sky is the limit in high jumping. This is because you can keep jumping and go higher and higher until you knock down the bar. The bar is raised higher each round during a competition. It continues to be raised until all but one jumper has been eliminated. The winner is the last remaining jumper. You get as many jumps as it takes until there is only one jumper left. When there are many good jumpers, the competition may go on for hours. Top high jumpers need good technique, but they also have to have endurance and the ability to keep concentrating.

This event has a long history. In Africa, many centuries ago, there were high jumping contests. They later became

In 1987 Patrik Sjoberg (Sweden) jumped 2.42m, higher than anyone had ever jumped before.

S. Kostadinova (Bulgaria) uses the *Fosbury flop* technique to clear the high jump.

Dick Fosbury (USA) developed a new technique to win the Olympic gold medal at Mexico in 1968.

part of the ancient Greek Olympics. Much more recently, in the mid-1800s, these contests were started again in England. Not long afterwards, an Englishman named Marshall Brooks became the first person ever to jump higher than six feet (1.83 m). The record rose again when Sweden's Patrik Sjoberg jumped 2.42 m (7 ft 11 in) in Stockholm in 1987.

A Russian named Igor Paklin raised the men's record to 2.41 m in 1985. He used the jumping technique called the Fosbury flop. The flop is named after the American jumper Dick Fosbury who used it when he won the Olympic high jumping gold medal in Mexico in 1968. He was the first jumper to use this way of jumping successfully. To try the Fosbury flop yourself, you must have your trainer with you. When you run up to the crossbar, turn as you go, so that when you arrive at the bar your back is facing it. Jump over the bar back first, arching your back and bending your knees so they do not touch the crossbar. Land shoulder first on a mattress. You have to have a well-padded landing area to do the flop. Not many people thought flopping was a good way of jumping when Dick Fosbury first used it. They thought he was good at it, but that it was not a very efficient way of jumping. Now the Fosbury flop is used by most of the top international high jumpers.

Another popular method is the straddle in which you clear the bar face down. This is how to do the straddle. Run up to the bar and take-off by kicking one leg over. Go over head first, with your stomach facing the bar. It looks like you are draping yourself around it.

At the 1932 Los Angeles Olympics, long before Dick Fosbury was even born, Mildred 'Babe' Didrikson dived over the bar. She and her last remaining opponent in the competition jumped higher than any woman ever had before. But Babe's way of high jumping was unusual at the time and in the final round was declared illegal by the judges. Surprisingly, instead of disqualifying her, they decided instead to award her second place and a joint world record with the winner. Now Babe's way of high jumping is accepted although it is no longer used much. It is known as 'the Western roll'. In athletics, as in the rest of life, what is considered acceptable can change.

All high jumpers take off by pushing off from one foot. You get three attempts at each height. You have to concentrate on lifting your hips at take-off and keeping your pelvis tilted forward. A fast approach run is not vital, but you

Having jumped so high it is important for the high jumper to land safely on sturdy crash mats. You should never attempt a high jump without a proper safety mat.

do need a natural ability to protect yourself at high vertical distances.

If you are interested in competing seriously in the high jump, you will need to train about four times a week, one hour per session. This can go up to about 1½ hours for 14- and 15-year-olds. You will need rest days between your sessions. Your training should include jumps, sprints, especially on an uphill slope, as well as playing other games like basketball and volleyball which involve jumping.

4.02m

15°   15°

18m

A high jump and approach area with dimensions.

Between each athlete's attempt at the high jump, officials check and alter the height of the bar and make sure it is correctly positioned.

Long Jump

You need a fast approach in the long jump. It really is a sprint with a high jump at the end of it. The winner is the athlete who jumps furthest forward. You land on the seat of your shorts. What you don't want to do is fall backwards after you land in the sand, because your jump is measured by the dent you have made in the sand. The nearest point is taken as the length you have jumped. Speed and precision on the long run-up are important. You have to be running at full speed when you 'hit' the eight inch wide (20 cm) wooden take-off board. A top jumper will usually change the rhythm of his or her last three strides to get a powerful take-off.

Two techniques now in use are the one-and-a-half stride hitch kick and the hang. In the hitch kick, after you take-off, you sweep one leg out and back as though you were cycling. As you begin to drop toward the sand pit you bring the other leg, the one you took off on, forward bent at the knee. You end up ready for landing with both legs bent and your arms over your head pointing forward. In the hang method, immediately after you take-off, you just 'hang' in the air with your legs stretched out. One trick just before landing is to stretch out both feet in front of you to gain some extra distance.

You get six trials at most, and you must not step on the take-off line. You will need training similar to the high jumper's, with more emphasis on sprinting. The long jump dates back to ancient Greece. The first long jumper whose distance has been recorded was an athletically gifted Spartan called Chionis. In 708 BC, he jumped 23 feet, 1½ inches (7.05 m). In modern times, the world record has moved up very slowly. After the American athlete, Jesse Owens, set a new world record of 8.13 m, in 1935, no one was able to jump farther for 25 years and 79 days. That is the longest time a world record in a standard event has ever remained unbroken.

Long jump officials measure the distance an athlete has jumped and prepare the pit for the next jumper.

A long jump pit and runway with dimensions.

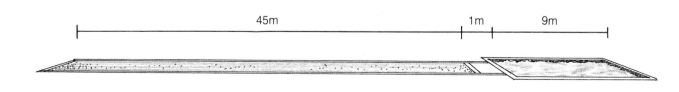

45m   1m   9m

Then, at the 1968 Olympics, Bob Beamon made an astonishing jump that has also proved very hard to beat. This tall New Yorker began his run-up, hit the board, and jumped, landing 8.9 m from the start. It was not only a new world record, it was more than 0.6 m longer than anybody had ever jumped. Beamon said, 'I still can't quite believe I jumped that far.' He had though. He set the new world record in Mexico City, which is high above sea level. Altitude is known to help in such events. He was also helped by the maximum allowable wind.

Another American genius at long jump, Carl Lewis, has emerged in the 1980s. His 8.79 m best was second only to Beamon. But in 1987, the Soviet Robert Emmiyan, 22, produced the second longest leap in history, 8.86 m. The woman who has become best known for the long jump is

Carl Lewis (USA) throws his body forward powerfully to achieve the longest possible jump.

Anisoara Stanciu. She is Romanian. She began jumping when she was 11, achieving 3.8 m. She cleared 6 m for the first time when she was 18. Although she pumps her arms a lot and over-strides on the run-up, she had won the 1984 Olympic title and set four world records by the time she was 23.

But who knows what would have happened at the 1984 Olympics if the East Germans had come and Heike Drechsler had competed. She is an all-round athlete, who first broke Stanciu's world long jump record in Berlin and then she took the record even higher with a jump of 24 feet 5½ inches (7.45 m) in Russia, in the summer of 1986.

Triple Jump

In the summer of 1985, under a blue Indiana sky, the long-legged American triple jumper Willie Banks leapt 58 feet 11½ inches (17.97 m). It was a new world record. The previous record, which had been set at altitude, in Mexico City, had stood for ten years. What made Willie Banks's achievement even greater was that he did not have the aid of altitude. If you were to watch Willie Banks leap, you would see that this event requires a hop, step and jump. Some historians think the triple jump is related to the game of hopscotch, which goes back more than 150 years. It is possible that the children's game was developed from the jumping event, or vice versa.

But the triple jump takes a lot of skill. Triple jumpers tend to be slower than long jumpers, but they have tremendous leg power. The take-off is entirely different. The triple jumper leaves the board with as much horizontal speed as possible, whereas the long jumper is trying to get distance through height. You have to take the hop and skip with the same leg, and the jump with the other. When you hop, you land on the same foot. Then you take a step with this foot,

A triple jumper with the hop, step and jump sequence. The dark red shoe shows the take off foot used for the hop and the step. The pink shoe shows the foot used for the jump.

In 1985, Willie Banks (USA) took a hop, step and jump to break the world record at the triple jump.

but end up standing on the other foot. For the jump, you take off from the same foot you are already standing on. You try to link these movements smoothly and jump as far as possible. As in the long jump, you land in sand.

In competition, everyone gets three jumps, and the best eight jumpers get three more. The order you start in is determined by lot. All jumps are measured from the nearest mark in the landing area made by any part of your body or limbs. You will need plenty of weight training and bounding to build the strength and resilience the triple jump requires. The triple jump has not yet been done by many women. It is a fairly new event at American colleges, and Wendy Brown set a 44 feet 6¾ inch (13.58 m) record in 1985. Because it is a new event, there are not yet many top women triple jumpers. For this reason, the world record is regarded as soft. In other words, it will not be hard to raise it higher and higher if more women take up the sport.

Pole Vault

Our ancestors invented pole vaulting for a very practical purpose. It was a way of crossing streams where there was no bridge. The vaulter ran towards the stream carrying a long pole, planted the pole and leapt into the air, coming to the ground on the other side of the stream. This was not only useful, it was fun. So, 2,000 years ago people began to have pole-vaulting competitions. The first ones took place in Ireland.

What has changed most in this sport over the centuries is the kind of pole you use. In the middle of the 19th century, Hugh H. Baxter, the first North American champion used a wooden pole weighing about 30 lbs (13.6 kg). In England at that time, in a region called the Lake District, the 'flying men' of Ulverston used an even heavier pole. These poles were made of ash, walnut or fir wood with a metal cap at the bottom end. Then came the age of bamboo. With lighter, more flexible poles, jumps soon rose. In 1883, Hugh Baxter

Pole vaulters use a long, flexible, glass fibre pole to vault their bodies high into the air and over a cross-bar.

tried a bamboo pole and surprised himself with a vault of more than eleven feet (3.65 metres). After World War Two pole vaulting entered the age of steel. These steel poles were strong but they could bend up to three feet without breaking.

Now we are in the age of glass fibre. The records started to go up as soon as we entered it. Because glass fibre poles are very light and flexible, they put spring into your vault. You can grip them higher up than you can metal poles. Even so beginners often find metal poles good to start with.

A pole vaulter has to combine the skills of a gymnast, an acrobat, and an athlete. You carry the pole at your side with the tip just a little higher, roughly in line with the top of your head. You carry the pole as high as you can, you run as fast as you can, then you plant the pole in a box or tin at the foot of the jump, and hang on. The pole bends under your weight, but shouldn't break. You are catapulted through the air over a bar. You have to clear the bar without knocking it down.

How you land depends on the kind of landing area. If it is a built-up foam pit, you can land however you want, but if the landing area is sand, you should take the weight off your legs before rolling over. In training, you have to learn to ride the pole. Using gym climbing ropes to swing and sit on a high pommel horse or box can help. Handstands and other such

A pole vault and pole with dimensions.

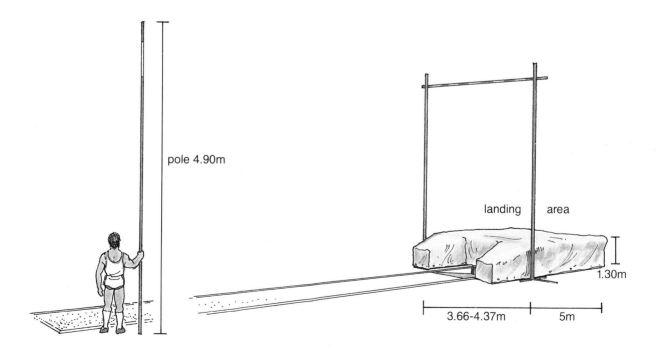

pole 4.90m

landing area

1.30m

3.66-4.37m   5m

gymnastic exercises will help too. How high is it possible to vault? No one knows. For a long time people thought no one would ever successfully vault as high as 6 metres (19ft 8¼ in). Then a Russian named Sergey Bubka did it in Paris in 1985. He said, 'I will go higher.' Since then he has.

Sergey Bubka (USSR) clears over 6m in the pole vault.

Multiple events

Who are the greatest athletcs in the world? Decathletes and heptathletes say it has to be them. They point out that their sport is an all-round event. To do it, they have to master far more events than anyone else does. They run, jump, and throw. But athletes who specialize in a single event are usually better at it than the multi-event athlete is. A world champion hepthalete, for example, will not be as good at shot putting as the shot put world champion is. Versatility is only one of the skills you need to be successful in these *multiple-events*. Because there are so many different events involved, you need plenty of stamina and strength and perseverence.

Athletes taking part in multiple events need to be good at both track and field athletics.

Decathlon (Ten Events)

The decathlete takes part in ten events over two days. The first day begins with a 100 m run, a test of speed. This is followed by the long jump. Then comes putting the shot. There is no official break for food, but at this point, most athletes grab a bite, usually something that is easily digested. Then they go on to the high jump, always a long, drawn-out competition. The last event of the day is the 400 m race – it is one lap of the track and must be run at full speed.

Day two begins with another race, the 110 m hurdles. Next the decathlete gets three attempts at throwing the discus. The pole vault follows. Then comes javelin throwing, and finally, a 1,500 m race. This middle distance race is really a challenge, and not just because by this time the athletes are tired. Most 1,500 m runners are lighter than decathletes have to be if they are to do well at the throwing events and if they are to have the muscle power to sprint through the 100 m. You get points for each event and the highest total wins.

Decathlon	
100 m	
Long jump	
Shot put	1st day
High jump	
400 m	
110 m hurdles	
Discus	
Pole vault	2nd day
Javelin	
1,500 m	

Jackie Joyner-Kersee (USA) competes in seven events in the heptathlon.

Heptathlon (Seven Events)

The heptathlete takes part in seven events over two days and is an event for women only. On the first day she has four events, and starts with a 100 m hurdle race. Next she puts the shot. Then comes the long, drawn-out high jump competition. The last event of her day is another running event, the 200 m race. It must be run flat out. If she has pushed herself hard, as is necessary for success, she will feel

(opposite page) Torsten Voss (GDR) has emerged as a decathlon champion in the late 1980's.

exhausted. But there is more to come on the second day. The day begins with the long jump. Then comes the javelin, finishing with an 800 m race. You get points for each event. The highest total wins. In Los Angeles, in 1984, an Australian named Glynnis Nunn became the first Olympic heptathlon champion. But the American heptathlete Jackie Joyner-Kersee was soon ranked highest in the world, and in 1986, in Texas, she set a record of 7,161 points.

Pentathlon (Five Events)

The pentathlon used to consist of five events. The first pentathlon event to be held at the Olympics was in 1964. The events held on the first day were 100 m hurdles, shot put and high jump. On the second day the long jump and 200 m were held. After the first four events only the leading group of competitors went forward to the last event. The 200 m was changed to 800 m in 1976, to provide a more demanding test. In 1980 it was decided to replace the pentathlon with the heptathlon and the event no longer takes place.

Heptathlon	
100 m hurdles	
Shot put	1st day
High jump	
200 m	
Long jump	
Javelin	2nd day
800 m	

Pentathlon	
100 m hurdles	
Shot put	1st day
High jump	
Long jump	2nd day
200 m	

Mary Peters (GB) won the Pentathlon Olympic Gold medal at Munich, Germany in 1972.

Clothes and equipment

Shoes

Shoes are the most important equipment in athletics. You can make do with ordinary clothing if necessary, but you should not skimp on shoes. They should fit well. If you can, get the shoes designed especially for your event. Your coach or physical education teacher can advise you on this. Discus shoes are flat with very thin heels. Pole vaulting shoes have a slightly wedged heel. Javelin boots are a bit like boxing boots but sturdier and they have long spikes front and back. Decathletes will need up to six different kinds of shoes in order to have the right ones for all ten events of the decathlon. You should wash your sport shoes with soap and water. An old tooth brush will help get them clean. Putting them in the washing machine will wear them out sooner and may shrink them. You should avoid drying leather-spiked shoes on a radiator – heat shrinks them.

Any athlete needs to wear the correct shoes for their event. It is very important that the shoes fit well and feel comfortable.

Clothes

The main point about the clothing you will wear for training is that is should be big enough and designed to give you freedom of movement. You want to feel at ease in your kit. You will usually compete in shorts and a tee shirt or singlet, but you will need warm-ups too. This includes a sweatshirt, sometimes with a hood attached, and tracksuit bottoms, which are good to train in, except in very hot weather. It is

Patrik Sjoberg (Sweden) wears a comfortable tracksuit for his training exercises that help him in the high jump.

convenient if these tracksuit bottoms have long zips at the ankles so you can take them off without having to remove your shoes. Be sure to keep warm. You will perform better if you feel comfortable and you will be less likely to get injured. Injuries often occur when your muscles are cold. Try to avoid long intervals of standing or sitting around during a training session because this can lead to chills. A light-weight, shower-proof tracksuit is a good investment if you live in a climate where it rains.

Jackie Joyner-Kersee (USA) wears shorts and tee shirt during competition.

Equipment

Your school or athletics club should be able to supply all the athletics equipment you will need to begin with. Eventually you may want to have your own. Top level pole vaulters, for example, have at least two or three fibreglass vaulting poles. Depending on your event, you may eventually get your own javelin, discus, shot or hammer. These all have to be regulation size, so be sure to get them from a reputable dealer.

Electronic scoreboards are used to display the results of the different events.

Important competitions

Olympic Games

Winning a gold medal at the Olympics is still the peak of athletic achievement. It is not certain, though, that it will always be.

Because of a political dispute that was not about sport, the USA decided to boycott the 1980 Olympic Games, which were being held in Moscow. Many Western nations also boycotted. Then, when the 1984 Olympic Games were held in Los Angeles, the USSR and many of its allies boycotted. Many people have hoped that that will be the end of the boycotts.

The Olympics are held every four years. There are summer games and winter games, but the summer ones, which include athletics, get the most attention. Until 1983, the Olympic champion was also regarded officially as the world champion. This was changed when athletics got its first world championships.

World championships

The world athletics championships have only been in existence since 1983. They were first held in Helsinki. Four years later, in 1987, the second world championships took

1896	Athens, Greece		
1900	Paris, France		
1904	St Louis, USA		
1908	London, England		
1912	Stockholm, Sweden		
1916	not held owing to war	1956	Melbourne, Australia
1920	Antwerp, Belgium	1960	Rome, Italy
1924	Paris, France	1964	Tokyo, Japan
1928	Amsterdam, Holland	1968	Mexico City, Mexico
1932	Los Angeles, USA	1972	Munich, West Germany
1936	Berlin, Germany	1976	Montreal, Canada
1940	not held owing to war	1980	Moscow, USSR
1944	not held owing to war	1984	Los Angeles, USA
1948	London, England	1988	Seoul, South Korea
1952	Helsinki, Finland	1992	Barcelona, Spain

The modern Olympic Games (dates and venues).

place in Rome. These championships are held every four years, one year before the Olympics. Whoever wins an event becomes the world champion in his or her event. This means that in every athletics event, there is now another title which is rivalling the Olympics in importance.

The World Student Games do not get as much attention but they are a preview of who is likely to become best in the world in later years.

The 1987 World Championships were held at the Rome Olympic stadium. Floodlights allow events to take place after day light has faded.

Other championships

Because the USA is such a big country with so many athletes, the *American Championships* are often a good indicator of who to look out for at the Olympics or World Championships. The winner in each event is the national champion. Most countries have national titles too, as well as national junior and school titles, regional and county titles at all levels.

The opening ceremonies are an important part of athletic championships. These ceremonies have become more and more spectacular as host countries try hard to impress people in the stadium or watching on television. Here a fly past by aircraft with smoke flares creates a colourful sight.

Every two years there are *European Championships*. The first ones took place in 1934. Women's events were included in 1946. They are what European athletes peak for between the Olympics and the World Championships. The first *Europa Cup* took place in 1965. It is considered important too by athletes who live in Europe, and now it is held every two years, in odd years. The Eastern European nations hold games called the *Spartakiad* and there are *Pan American Games* for countries of North and South America.

The *Commonwealth Games* are for athletes from all over the British Commonwealth. The first games were held in 1930 in Hamilton, Canada. At the second Games, in London, England, women competed for the first time. The thirteenth Games in Edinburgh in 1986, however, were not considered a success. Many African nations boycotted these Games because they did not agree with British policy on South Africa.

The spectators at an event play an important part in encouraging athletes to greater achievements.

Getting into competition

It is usually possible to start by competing at school. You may also want to join a local club. Your physical education teacher or coach, or someone who coaches at a nearby sports centre, can probably direct you to the right club and help you enter your first competition.

If not, your national athletics organization will send details of clubs year you. It is a good idea to tell them your age when you write and send a stamped, addressed envelope. (Useful Addresses are listed near the end of this book.)

There are frequent competitions for boys and girls aged eleven and up. Many clubs participate in competitions at club, local and county level.

The Olympic flag of five linked coloured rings and the Olympic flame – symbols of world friendship.

Famous stadiums

Crystal Palace

The track at Crystal Palace, which is the British National Sports Centre, is the home of British athletics. It is on the southern outskirts of London. Its first synthetic surface was built in 1968.

An athletics stadium showing the field area.

Pole-vault

Floodlights

High jump

Crash mats

Throwing areas

Electronic scoreboard

Javelin

Hammer and Discus

Long jump

Shot put

Running track

Bislett

This stadium in Oslo, Norway, draws athletes from around the world. A statue of the famous marathoner Grete Weitz, who pioneered women's long distance running, was put up even while she was still at her peak. This is a rare honour at a stadium which has seen many rare feats.

The Coliseum

The Los Angeles Coliseum hosted the 1984 Olympics. It also staged the 1932 Games. It is notoriously windy. Los Angeles is also known for its polluted air, which is not good for athletics. The Coliseum's synthetic Rekortan track was laid in 1983.

Glossary

Anabolic steroids Synthetic male hormones which are used to stimulate muscle and bone growth. They have dangerous side-effects and are banned.

Cage The C-shaped cage erected around the hammer and discus throwing circle for safety.

Callisthenics Bodily exercises done without the use of apparatus or with light hand apparatus, used to develop grace and co-ordination or to 'loosen-up' muscles before participating in other strenuous activities.

Coach Person responsible for the training and motivation of an athlete.

Decathlon An all-round track and field event for men, held over two days. Day one: 100 m, long jump, shot, high jump and 400 m. Day two: 110 m hurdles, discus, pole vault, javelin and 1500 m. Points are awarded for each of the ten events.

Fosbury flop The technique of high jumping in which you clear the bar on your back. It is named after Dick Fosbury who used it at the 1968 Olympics.

Hang A style of long-jumping in which the body is extending in flight to end up in a good landing position.

Heptathlon An all-round track and field event for women held over two days. Day 1: 100 m hurdles, high jump, shot, 200 m. Day 2: long jump, javelin, 800 m. Points are awarded for each of the seven events.

IAAF The governing body of athletics. The initials stand for International Amateur Athletic Federation. The IAAF authorises world records and makes the rules.

No jump An illegal long or triple jump.

O'Brien In the shot put, the method of starting with your back facing the direction of put. It is widely used now, and was developed by Parry O'Brien, an American who was the Olympic champion of 1952 and 1956.

Pain barrier The physical pain an athlete may have to overcome during training and competition.

Pentathlon An all-round women's track and field event made up of five events held over two days.

Plant In the pole vault, to place the pole in the box before you vault.

Psychological barrier A level of achievement most people think is impossible until someone actually attains it. This lack of confidence makes it hard to attain. The barrier of the 6 m pole vault fell in 1985 partly because Sergey Bubka, who accomplished it, believed it could be done.

Put The method of hurling the shot. It is more a push than a throw and the shot is held close to your neck.

Scratch line The line you must not cross at the end of the javelin, long jump and triple jump runway.

Stopboard The wooden board at the front of the shot put circle. It helps stop the athlete from moving forward. You are not allowed to touch the top of the board.

Straddle The technique of high jumping in which you take off from the foot nearer the bar, cross face down, and roll over it, landing on your back.

Weight training Exercising with free weights or Nautilus and other machines. This builds strength.

Further reading

World Sporting Records by David Emery and Stan Greenberg (Bodley Head, 1986)
Daley Thompson: The Subject is winning by Skip Rozin (Stanley Paul, 1983)
Tessa: My life in athletics by Tessa Sanderson (Willow, 1986)
The Olympians by Sebastian Coe (Pavilion, 1984)

Foul Play: Drug Abuse in Sports by Tom Donohoe and Neil Johnson (Basil Blackwell, 1986)
Grace Under Pressure: The emergence of women in sport by Adrianne Blue (Sidgwick & Jackson, 1987)
Guinness book of Olympic Records by Stan Greenberg (Guinness, 1987)

Useful addresses

Amateur Athletics Association
Francis House
Francis Street
London
SW1P 1DE

Australian Athletic Union
710–722 Mount Alexander Road
Moonee Ponds
Melbourne
Victoria
3039
Australia

New Zealand Amateur Athletic Association
P.O. Box 741
Wellington
New Zealand

Sports Council
16 Upper Woburn Place
London
WC1

Canadian Track & Field Association
355 River Road
Tower B
Vanier City
Ottawa
Ontario
KIL 8C1

Athletics Congress of USA
P.O. Box 120
Indianapolis
Indiana
46206–0120
USA

Index

figures in **bold** refer to illustrations